Become a Woman Billionaire:

A Complete Guide to Women's Financial Freedom

By

Marie J. Garcia

TABLE OF CONTENT

INTRODUCTION

As we enter a new era of progress and equality, women are proving themselves as leaders, innovators, and entrepreneurs like never before. Yet, despite the advances in gender parity, the gender wealth gap persists, with women still trailing behind men in terms of financial independence and success.

But what if we told you that it doesn't have to be that way? What if we told you that you, as a woman, have the power and potential to become a billionaire and achieve financial freedom on your own terms?

In "Become a Woman Billionaire: A Complete Guide to Women's Financial Freedom," we present a groundbreaking roadmap for women to unlock their full financial potential and join the ranks of the world's most successful businesswomen.

Drawing on decades of research, experience, and interviews with some of the most successful female entrepreneurs and investors, this book provides a comprehensive and actionable guide for women at any stage of their financial journey, whether you're just starting out or already have an established business.

From building a solid financial foundation to finding the right business idea, from negotiating like a pro to building a winning team, from managing risk to investing wisely, we cover everything you need to know to build and grow a successful business that can generate billions in revenue and wealth.

But this book isn't just about accumulating wealth; it's about using that wealth to create positive change in the world, to empower other women, and to leave a lasting legacy.

So, whether you're a young woman just starting out in your career, a seasoned entrepreneur looking to take your business to the next level, or simply someone who wants to take control of their finances and build a better future, "Become a Woman Billionaire" is the ultimate guide to financial freedom for women.

CHAPTER 1

Create a Mentality of Abundance for Yourself

Establishing a wealth mindset is the first thing that has to be done in order to reach the goal of gaining financial independence.

When it comes to achieving financial independence as a woman, cultivating a wealth mindset is absolutely necessary. In spite of the fact that women have made significant headway in recent years with regard to gender equality and pay parity, the undeniable fact remains that women continue to face a distinct set of monetary obstacles. Studies have shown that women are more likely to live longer than males and to take on more caregiving tasks, all of which might impair a person's potential to generate wealth. Additionally, women tend to earn less money than men.

Developing a wealth mindset, on the other hand, might be of assistance to women in overcoming these obstacles and achieving financial independence.

Alterations in one's mentality that are essential for the accumulation of riches

Changing one's mentality substantially is necessary in order to accumulate wealth as a woman. Throughout the course of history, women have been excluded from the process of making financial decisions and have faced systemic impediments to the building of wealth. In spite of this, the times are shifting, and there are currently more options available to women than ever before to amass wealth and ensure their financial stability in the future. The following are some of the most significant modifications in mentality that women need to make in order to accumulate wealth:

Believe in Yourself

One of the most essential transformations in mentality that women need to make is to have faith in themselves and their capacity to amass financial success. Imposter syndrome is a common condition that affects women and might prevent them from taking chances and moving forward with their ambitions. It is crucial to keep in mind that you are capable of reaching financial success and that you have abilities and talents that are worthwhile to offer. Remembering this will be very helpful.

A willingness to take risks is essential.

Increasing one's fortune necessitates executing some moderately risky actions. Women frequently avoid taking chances because they are afraid of failing or suffering the repercussions of doing something wrong. However, it is essential to keep in mind that even the most successful people have fallen short of their goals at some point in their lives. You can get priceless experience and learn from your failures if you are willing to take some risks and play the odds.

Prioritize Financial Education

Building money requires a solid foundation in financial literacy. Learning about personal economics, investing, and business ownership should be at the forefront of women's educational priorities. Education in the area of finance can assist women in making educated choices regarding their finances and avoiding costly errors. There is a wealth of resources accessible, such as in-person and online workshops, as well as printed books.

Develop a number of different sources of revenue.

Establishing several avenues of financial support is necessary in order to amass wealth. Women should search for chances to diversify their income streams, such as launching a side hustle, investing in real estate, or creating a passive income stream through investing, and they should look for these alternatives. Women have the ability to boost their earning potential and establish a financial safety net for themselves if they have various sources of income.

Adopt a perspective that is more long-term.

Increasing one's fortune is a process that takes a lot of time. When it comes to their finances, women should have patience and adopt a perspective that is focused on the long term. It is essential to keep in mind that accumulating wealth is a process that takes time and requires ongoing work. Women have the potential to achieve great financial success over time if they direct their attention to the achievement of long-term goals and make investments on a regular, albeit modest, basis.

Establish a Strong Base of Support

The process of amassing riches can be difficult at times, but it is noticeably less difficult when one has a support system. Women need to surround themselves with individuals who are positive about their ability to achieve their financial objectives and who cheer them on when they do. People such as friends, family members, mentors, and financial advisors can fall under this category.

Conquer your anxieties and challenge your limiting beliefs.
Women can be held back by their own fears and limiting views.

CHAPTER 2

Financial Goals

As a woman, it is imperative that you take care of your finances and prepare for your future in order to achieve financial independence and security. Setting financial goals is a vital component of obtaining financial security and independence. Setting financial goals will assist you in achieving your financial objectives and building a solid financial foundation, regardless of whether you are beginning a job, getting married, having a family, or planning for retirement. Setting financial goals may be done at any stage of life.

The significance of determining your financial objectives, the actions you may take to determine and accomplish your financial objectives, and a few suggestions for achieving success as a woman are covered in this article.

Why Should You Establish Financial Goals?

It is vital to set financial goals for a number of reasons, including the following:

Putting together a strategy for your future: Regardless of whether your target is to purchase a home, launch a business, or save money for retirement, setting financial goals can assist you in developing a strategy that will lead to your success.

Motivation: If you have a specific plan laid out for how you want your money to be spent, it will be easier for you to stay motivated and focused on reaching your goals. Setting financial objectives can help you build a firm financial foundation and provide a safety net in the event of unexpected events such as illness, job loss, or emergency. Financial security can be achieved by the setting of financial goals.

Empowerment: Taking responsibility of your finances and creating financial goals can help you feel more in control of your financial future and empower you to make educated financial decisions. Taking charge of your finances and setting financial goals can help you feel more in control of your financial future.

A Guide to Establishing Your Financial Objectives

Find out what your financial goals are: The first thing you need to do in order to achieve your financial goals is to find out what your financial goals are. What are some of your goals with regard to your finances? Do you want to get out from under your debt, put money away for a down payment on a property, or launch your own company? Make your goals Specific, Measurable, Achievable, Relevant, and Time-bound are the components that make up the acronym SMART. Be sure that your goals satisfy these requirements in order to make them more attainable. Make a budget: Making a budget can assist you in locating areas of your spending that may be reduced, allowing you to reallocate the saved money toward the accomplishment of your monetary objectives.

Set your goals in order of importance: Determine which of your goals are the most important to you, and then arrange the others in descending order of importance. Keep an eye on your advancement: Keeping an eye on your advancement toward your financial goals can assist you stay encouraged and enable you to make adjustments as required.

Understanding your temperance dealing with money

The first step toward achieving financial stability and success as a woman is to gain an understanding of the type of relationship you have with money. Your ideas, attitudes, behaviors, and habits in relation to money make up what is known as your "money personality." Your upbringing, the events and experiences of your life, your cultural heritage, and the norms of society all contribute to the formation of your identity. Discovering your money personality can assist you in improving the judgments you make regarding your finances, enhancing your overall financial well-being, and realizing your financial ambitions.

The following is a list of common money personalities that can be found in women:

The one who places an emphasis on saving money and adhering to a financial plan is known as a saver. They would rather spend less than they earn in order to build up their wealth over time. They typically exercise restraint when it comes to spending money and steer clear of making rash acquisitions. People who save money are typically very conscientious about keeping track of their expenditures, establishing financial goals, and developing a spending plan.

Spenders, also known as spendthrifts, are people who take pleasure in frivolous spending and put a high value on experiencing satisfaction in the here and now. They have a tendency to have a more laid-back perspective on money and may not be as disciplined when it comes to saving or creating a budget. A spendthrift is someone who makes impulsive purchases frequently and may have problems with overspending or debt.

The avoider is a person who experiences feelings of being overwhelmed by the management of their finances and as a result, avoids dealing with those issues altogether. They may feel shame or guilt about their financial condition, have a negative attitude toward money, or lack confidence in their capacity to properly handle money. Another possibility is that they lack confidence in their ability to manage money efficiently.

A person who worries about their financial situation is someone who suffers from anxiety or stress due to their finances. It's possible that they're plagued by persistent anxiety about their financial future and that they have trouble making decisions that include money. People who worry a lot may have a propensity to be overly cautious or risk-averse, which can restrict the chances available to them financially.

The investor Investors are those who are interested in accumulating wealth through various forms of investment. It's possible that they have a solid understanding of the financial markets, various investment vehicles, and various tactics for risk management. Investors typically have self-control, patience, and a focus on the achievement of long-term objectives.

Your money personality as a woman may be shaped in some ways by society expectations, gender roles, and cultural standards, to name a few of these potential influences. For instance, women may be socialized to emphasize the needs of others over their own financial objectives, which can lead to undersaving or neglecting their own financial well-being. Men, on the other hand, may be socialized to favor their own financial goals over the needs of others. There is a gender wage difference, work disruptions owing to caring responsibilities, and greater healthcare expenditures, all of which can have an impact on women's capacity to maintain their financial security. In addition, women may face other special problems.

Recognizing and overcoming self-limiting ideas regarding financial matters

In order to achieve monetary success and independence as a woman, it is essential to acknowledge the limiting views that you hold about money and to overcome those beliefs. Negative ideas or attitudes can be limiting beliefs. They prevent us from realizing our full potential and achieving our goals. Our upbringing, cultural conditioning, previous experiences, and even the messages we receive from the media can all contribute to the formation of these views. When it comes to money, limiting beliefs can be especially harmful because they can prohibit us from achieving our financial objectives and realizing our true earning potential. These beliefs can also keep us from being happy with our current financial situation.

It might be tough to notice limiting attitudes about money since they may be so embedded in one's thought process that they are difficult to spot. On the other hand, some common instances of restricting ideas around money that women may hold include the following:

The misconception that women are not adept with money and are unable to make sound decisions regarding their finances.

A belief that putting one's own wants and needs in terms of one's finances ahead of those of others is selfishness.

The notion that being affluent or successful financially is incompatible with a woman's gender.

The idea that in order to be successful financially, one must either put in a lot of long hours or give up things that bring them joy.

The idea that wealth itself is sinful or that having a lot of money is in some way responsible for all of society's ills.

The conviction that one's current economic circumstances are predetermined by variables such as one's upbringing or social standing.

It is imperative that you examine the restrictive beliefs you have towards money. These convictions may be deeply established and may have been formed over the course of time as a result of a variety of life experiences and the standards of society. However, putting these assumptions to the test is essential to achieving financial success and gaining financial empowerment.

The following is a list of common limiting attitudes that women may hold regarding money, as well as techniques to confront those assumptions:

"I'm not very good with handling money."
Many women have the misconception that they are not excellent with money or that they do not possess the abilities necessary to efficiently handle their cash.
This is one of the most widely held beliefs, and its origins may be traced all the way back to childhood. Many girls may not receive the same opportunity as males to learn about how to handle their money or receive instruction on how to become financially literate. As a direct consequence of this, some women may have the misconception that they are fundamentally terrible with money. On the other hand, this belief is not correct. This

misconception might cause a lack of self-assurance, which in turn can lead to avoiding financial planning and management. However, if one has access to the appropriate education and resources, they can teach themselves how to efficiently handle their finances.

Starting with reading books, going to workshops, enrolling in classes, and educating yourself on fundamental financial concepts like budgeting, saving, and investing is a good place to begin started challenging this idea. There is a plethora of information at one's disposal, such as books, online courses, and professional financial consultants. You may increase your financial literacy and get greater confidence in your ability to handle money management if you put in the effort to practice and educate yourself.

"Only men are allowed to have money."
Men have historically been portrayed as the key decision-makers and breadwinners in society, particularly in relation to financial matters. Because of this misconception, some women may have the impression that they do not have an equal position in the world of finance. Nevertheless, the truth is that women and men

have equal access to financial opportunities, and a significant number of successful women work in the financial sector.

Put yourself in the company of other successful women in the financial sector to dispute this perception. Keeping yourself motivated and focused on your financial goals and aspirations by surrounding yourself with others who believe in those goals and aspirations can be helpful. Seek out mentors or become a member of a group of other women who share your values and can provide you with support and encouragement.

"Money is the root of all evil."

This idea frequently has its origins in religious or cultural beliefs, which commonly connect riches with greed or immorality. However, money is merely a tool, and like any other instrument, it may be put to either positive or negative use. Each person is responsible for making their own choices regarding how they spend their own money. It is possible to utilize one's wealth to help those in need, to support causes that are in alignment with one's beliefs, and to guarantee a secure financial future for oneself and one's loved ones.

Changing the way that you think about money can be an effective way to counter this idea. Instead of viewing it as something negative, think of it as a resource that has the potential to be put to good use and have a positive effect on the world.

Self-care is a practice that can help women prioritize their own needs and aspirations, and lessen the feelings of guilt and shame that might come along with putting yourself first. Self-care can help women prioritize their own needs and goals. Setting limits, cultivating mindfulness, and participating in things that offer joy and fulfillment are all examples of what this can entail.

Seeking the counsel of a professional financial planner or advisor can assist women in developing a customized financial strategy and achieving their monetary objectives. This can be accomplished by seeking the advice of a professional. When women are faced with difficult financial situations, counseling and support from a professional can be quite helpful.

The fundamentals of female financial planning, including budgeting and saving

To be able to effectively manage her finances, a woman should work on developing essential skills such as saving money and creating a budget. Creating an accurate budget can assist you in reaching your monetary objectives, remaining within your financial limits, and providing you with a feeling of financial security. On the other side, saving allows you to amass wealth and construct a safety net for times when unexpected expenses arise.

Every woman ought to be familiar with the following fundamentals of financial planning and savings:

Be aware of both your income and your expenditures. In order to make a budget, you must first have an understanding of both your income and your expenses. Begin by making a list of all of the ways in which you bring in money, including your primary source of income as well as any additional sources of income you may have. Next, make a list of all of your expenses, including both set expenses like your rent or mortgage payments, utilities, insurance, and groceries, and variable expenses like going out to eat, going to the movies, and shopping.

When you have a complete inventory of all of your expenditures, the next step is to sort them into two categories: those that are important and those that are not essential. Non-essential expenses include things like entertainment, dining out, and shopping, whereas necessary expenses include things like housing, utilities, and groceries that you need to live. Essential expenses include things like these.

Establish a spending plan.
You will be able to construct a budget if you have an accurate grasp of both your income and your expenses. A plan that assists you in distributing your income among your expenses, savings, and assets, a budget is a type of plan. It is helpful in identifying areas in which you can reduce your spending and raise the amount of money you save.

In order to successfully develop a budget, the first step is to establish some financial goals. These objectives may be short-term objectives, such as paying off debt or putting money away for a trip, or they may be long-term objectives, such as purchasing a home, beginning a business, or putting money away for retirement. When you have a clear idea of what you want to accomplish, you can decide how to best put your earnings to use.

It is essential that you take the necessary steps to ensure that your expenditures do not go beyond your income. If you discover that your expenditures are greater than your income, you will need to search for places where you may make reductions in your spending.

Keep Tabs on Your Expenditures: Once you have a working budget in place, the next step is to keep tabs on your expenditures to ensure that you are remaining true to your budget. This can assist you identify areas in which you may be spending more than necessary so that you can make modifications in accordance with those findings.

Establish a Contingency Savings Account It is critical to maintain a contingency savings account that can cover unforeseen costs such as a medical bill or a repair on your vehicle. Your goal should be to have at least three to six months' worth of living expenses stashed away in an account that is simple to access.

Pay Off Your Debt: Debt with high interest rates, such that from credit cards, may be a big drain on your money if it is not paid off. Your top priority should be to pay off as much of your debt as quickly as you can by prioritizing the obligations with the highest interest rates and making additional payments whenever you are able.

Put Money Aside for Future Goals Once you've established an emergency fund and paid off your debt, it's time to start putting money aside for future goals, such as a down payment on a home, a retirement fund, or a vacation. Think about setting up individual savings accounts for each of your objectives so that you can easily monitor your progress toward achieving them.

Make sure that your goals for your budget and savings are attainable in light of the money that you bring in and the money that you spend. Avoid putting unnecessary pressure on yourself by having expectations that are too high.

Look for ways to lower your monthly expenses, such as getting rid of television, shopping around for cheaper insurance, or negotiating your bills. Look for ways to reduce your monthly expenses, such as getting rid of cable.

You can save more consistently if you automate your savings by setting up monthly transfers from your checking account to your savings account. This will ensure that you save on a regular basis.

Take advantage of the perks offered by your employer. If your business provides you with extra benefits or a retirement savings plan, you should take advantage of them so that you can save money for the future.

Get professional assistance: If you are having trouble getting your finances in order, you should think about working with a financial advisor or enrolling in a personal finance school so that you can learn more about creating a budget and saving money.

For women to reach a point of financial independence and stability, it is critical for them to acquire the skills necessary to create a budget and save money.

The significance of developing a spending plan.

To regain control of your financial situation, one of the most crucial things you can do is to make a budget and stick to it. Creating a budget can assist you in accomplishing your monetary objectives and laying a solid groundwork for your future, regardless of whether you are single, married, or a parent. The following are a few of the many reasons why it is essential for women to develop a budget.

You will be able to maintain control of your financial situation and make any required adjustments to your budget with the help of this. You should look for places where you can reduce your spending, such as eating out or going shopping, and then make an effort to find ways to save money in those places.

Plan for irregular expenses

It is vital to plan for irregular expenses in addition to your usual monthly expenses. Some examples of irregular expenses include medical bills, car repairs, and holiday gifts. Be sure that these costs are factored into your budget, and that you set aside money on a regular basis to cover them. This can assist you in avoiding unanticipated costs, which can throw a wrench into your financial plans.

Be flexible

Keep in mind that your spending plan is not carved in stone and that it may require revisions as your circumstances evolve. Maintain a flexible attitude toward your financial plan and be open to make adjustments as necessary. For instance, if you get a pay raise or begin generating more cash, you may be able to boost the amount that you put away in savings or allot more money toward spending on things that are optional.

Putting money aside for future use is a crucial part of personal finance, and women should make it a top priority. Nevertheless, it is not always simple to save money, and this is especially true for women, who confront specific hurdles like as the gender pay gap, job interruptions owing to the responsibilities of caregiving, and longer life expectancies. Despite this, women are able to triumph over these obstacles and accomplish their monetary objectives if they employ the appropriate tactics. The following is a list of efficient methods that women can use to save money:

Establish concrete objectives for your savings: The first thing you should do when learning how to save money is to establish objectives that are explicit and attainable. It is important for women to articulate their monetary goals and calculate the amount they will need to set aside each month to reach those goals. Among these objectives could include the establishment of an emergency fund, the elimination of debt, the accumulation of funds for a down payment on a property, or the funding of retirement accounts. After you have decided what you want to do, the next step is to devise a strategy for how much money you will need to put away on a monthly basis.

Keep tabs on your spending: If you want to cut costs and save money, you need to know where your money is going. Establishing a budget and keeping careful records of your spending might help you keep tabs on your finances. This will assist you in determining areas in which you can make reductions and so save money. You may get a better handle on your finances and keep track of your expenditures with the assistance of budgeting applications like Mint and YNAB.

Negotiate your payments. A lot of women spend too much money on monthly expenses like cable, internet, and phone services. It is essential to negotiate these bills in order to obtain the most favorable interest rates feasible. Make a phone call to each of your service providers and beg for a better rate; if that doesn't work, move to a cheaper provider.

Paying off debt is one of the most effective methods to save money, therefore reducing it should be one of your top priorities. Create a strategy for paying off your debts, and prioritize those obligations with the highest interest rates to be paid off first. If you want to save money on interest costs, you might think about consolidating your debt into a loan or credit card with a reduced interest rate.

Automate your savings: If you want to save money quickly and easily, one of the easiest things you can do is automate your saves. You should arrange for money to be sent from your checking account to your savings account on a monthly basis automatically. Because of this, you will be able to put money away before you even have the chance to spend it.

Shop savvily: Women who shop in a savvy manner can save money for themselves. Make the most of bargains and discounts by shopping at discount retailers, using coupons, and taking advantage of sales. When it comes to products that you use on a regular basis, such as toilet paper, cleaning supplies, and meals that do not perish, it is more cost effective to buy them in bulk.

Boost your income: Another way for women to cut costs and save money is to boost their income. Consider finding a side job or beginning a side hustle.
Putting Money Away for the Future

Making an investment in one's future is a step that is vital for everyone to take, but it is an especially crucial step for women. When it comes to financial planning and investment, women frequently confront distinct obstacles due to the cultural and sociological standards that prevail in their society. Women can, however, overcome these challenges and position themselves for a financially secure future by employing the appropriate tactics and adopting the appropriate mentality.

If a woman wants to make an investment in her future, she should keep the following things in mind:

Gain an understanding of the gender gap in wealth. The inequality in wealth that exists between men and women is referred to as the gender wealth gap. It is a recurrent problem that may be traced back to a number of factors, including salary inequity, job interruptions owing to the duties of caring for a family, and a lack of financial literacy. A study that was conducted by the National Institute on Retirement Security found that women had a probability that is 80 percentage points higher than that of men of being poor at age 65 or older.

Women might be more proactive about planning for their financial futures if they have a grasp of the wealth disparity between men and women. It is critical to have an awareness of the specific obstacles that women experience and to take action to lessen the effects of those challenges.

It is quite doubtful that this strategy will result in success over the long term. Instead, women should put their attention toward developing a diverse investment portfolio that is in line with their long-term monetary objectives.

Keep in mind that there is always the possibility of losing money when investing. Despite the fact that there are no guarantees in the world of investing, taking a long-term perspective can assist women in weathering the short-term ups and downs of the market and achieving their long-term financial objectives.

Think About Engaging the Services of a Financial Advisor

Working with a financial advisor can be an excellent method for women to obtain individualized counsel and help in the process of financial planning and investing. This can be a very beneficial option for women. A financial advisor may assist women in developing a thorough strategy for their financial future, locating possibilities for investment, and ensuring that they remain on track to achieve their long-term objectives.

When selecting a financial advisor, it is critical to search for someone who is not just knowledgeable but also trustworthy and whose values and objectives are congruent with your own. In addition, women should be ready to ask questions, have a firm grasp on the monetary goals they wish to achieve, and maintain an active role in the planning process.

It is essential for women who wish to close the wealth gap between themselves and their male counterparts and attain long-term financial security to make investments in their own future.

CHAPTER 3

Investments.

The process of investing is a vital component of sound financial planning, and investors can choose from a wide variety of opportunities to put their money to work. Every possible route for investing comes with its own distinct set of qualities as well as perks and drawbacks. If you have certain financial objectives that you want to accomplish, it is important to have a solid understanding of the different kinds of investments that are available to you so that you can attain those objectives.

The following is a list of some of the most prevalent kinds of investments:

Stocks

Increasing your wealth over time through the purchase of stocks is a common practice that has the potential to be quite profitable. When you buy stocks, you are essentially purchasing a piece of ownership in the firm that you are investing in. You will be able to see a return on your investment when the value of your shares goes up as a direct result of the growth and increased profitability of the company in which you have invested.

It is essential to have a thorough understanding of the dangers associated with stock trading before making any investments in the stock market. The price of a share of stock can be highly unpredictable, and there is no assurance that the value of a company's shares will always go up. Investing in stocks, on the other hand, can be an excellent method to generate wealth over the long run if you take the appropriate strategy and exercise some patience.

If you are considering making an investment in the stock market, here are some important factors to keep in mind:

Get organized by making a plan: It is essential to have a well-defined strategy in place before beginning to invest in stocks and other securities. Your investing timeframe, your level of comfort with taking risks, and your financial goals should all be included here. Do you intend to invest for the long term, or do you have your sights set on profits in the near future? Do you want to invest in certain stocks, or would you rather put your money into a diverse portfolio that includes a variety of investments in addition to equities? If you have a well-defined strategy in place, it will be easier for you to make well-informed decisions and continue moving forward in the direction of achieving your monetary objectives.

When you invest in stocks, it is crucial to conduct your research and choose firms that you believe will do well over the long term. This is especially true when choosing which companies to invest in. Look for businesses that have a demonstrated history of robust growth, robust financials, and a competitive advantage in the sector in which they operate. You can also do an analysis of a company's financials and track record online using a variety of tools and resources, in addition to examining industry trends and economic variables that may influence the company's performance.

Make sure you have a diversified portfolio, as this is one of the most important factors in successful investment. This necessitates the purchase of a wide range of equities, in addition to investments in other assets such as bonds, real estate, and commodities. If you invest your money in a variety of different asset classes, you can lower the overall risk of your portfolio and potentially achieve higher returns over the long term. You can also protect yourself against declines in any one market by diversifying your stock holdings across a variety of businesses and sectors. This can be accomplished through the practice of stock diversification.

Bonds

Bonds are consistently ranked among the most widely used investment vehicles available on the market for financial assets. Bonds are a type of investment with a fixed income that provide investors with the opportunity to receive a consistent stream of income in the form of interest payments in addition to the possibility of receiving capital appreciation if the market value of the bond grows.

In this lesson, we will go over what bonds are, how they operate, the many kinds of bonds that are accessible to investors, the potential benefits and drawbacks of investing in bonds, as well as the steps necessary to invest in bonds.

What exactly is a bond?

Bonds are a form of financial instrument that facilitate the borrowing of funds from investors by organizations such as corporations, governments, and other entities. When an investor acquires a bond, they are effectively lending money to the issuer of the bond in exchange for regular interest payments and the return of their initial investment when the bond matures.

How do bonds work?

Bonds come with a predetermined date of maturity, which is the time at which the issuer is required to return the principal amount invested by the investor. Depending on the type of bond, the date of maturity could be anywhere from a few months to several decades in the future.

Bonds have a fixed interest rate, which is the rate at which the issuer will pay interest to the investor. Depending on the kind of bond purchased, the rate of interest may either be set in stone or be subject to change.

Coupon payments are the interest payments that the issuer makes to the investor. These payments are known as coupons. Depending on the provisions of the bond, coupon payments are normally made either semi-annually or annually. However, the frequency of these payments might vary.

When a bond is first issued, it is placed on the primary market and offered for sale to potential investors. After then, it is eligible for trading on the secondary market, which is the marketplace where investors purchase and sell bonds to other investors.

There are many distinct kinds of bonds.
Bonds are a type of financial instrument that can be used to raise cash by a variety of entities, including corporations, governments, and other organizations. A bond can essentially be thought of as a debt that an investor gives to the entity that is issuing the bond. In return for the loan, the issuer makes a commitment to the investor that they will receive interest payments at a predetermined rate over a predetermined time period, and that they will be repaid the principal amount of the loan when the bond reaches its maturity date. There is a wide variety of each sort of link, and each carries with it a distinct set of qualities and dangers.

Treasury bonds are a type of bond that is issued by the United States government to raise money for the country's ongoing activities. Because they are supported by the whole confidence and financial might of the United States government, they are often regarded as the most secure kind of bond. Treasury bonds normally have maturities that range anywhere from ten to thirty years and pay interest every six months.

Bonds issued by corporations are known as corporate bonds. Corporations issue bonds in order to raise funds for their activities. Bonds issued by corporations can be further divided into two categories: investment-grade bonds and high-yield, sometimes known as trash, bonds. High-yield bonds, on the other hand, are issued by corporations with lower credit ratings and consequently involve a greater level of risk than investment-grade bonds. Investment-grade bonds are issued by companies that have solid credit ratings. Bonds issued by corporations often have maturities that range anywhere from one to thirty years and pay interest on a semiannual basis.

Municipal bonds are debt obligations that are issued by state and municipal governments to raise capital for the construction of public buildings and infrastructure, such as schools, highways, and hospitals. Because municipal bonds are not subject to federal income tax and may also not be subject to state or local income tax, they are an attractive investment option for investors who are in higher tax categories. Bonds issued by municipalities can be further divided into two categories: revenue bonds and general obligation bonds. Revenue bonds are supported by the revenue that is generated by the project that is being financed, in contrast to general obligation bonds, which are backed by the full faith and credit of the government that is issuing them.

Agency bonds are bonds that are issued to support the purchase of mortgages by government-sponsored firms such as Fannie Mae and Freddie Mac. These bonds are also known as mortgage-backed securities (MBS). Agency bonds are not directly guaranteed by the United States government, unlike Treasury bonds, therefore some people view them as carrying a somewhat higher level of risk. Despite this perception, however, agency bonds are still regarded as relatively secure investments.

Bonds issued in a currency other than the U.S. dollar are considered to be international bonds. These bonds might be issued by foreign governments or enterprises. Investors can reap the benefits of diversification when they purchase international bonds; nevertheless, these bonds come with the risk of currency fluctuation and the possibility that the issuing country would experience political and economic upheaval.

Bond investing can provide a variety of rewards; however, there is also the possibility of danger. Bonds are a type of debt security that can be issued by governments or organizations in order to raise money for various purposes. Bonds are purchased by investors as a means of generating a consistent income in the form of interest payments and also as a potential means of generating capital gains by selling the bond at a price that is greater than what they first paid for it.

The following are some advantages of bond investing:

Bonds provide a regular income in the form of interest payments, which can be cashed out at predetermined intervals. Because of this, they are an appealing choice for investors who are interested in receiving consistent income.

Lower risk: When compared to stocks, bonds are typically thought to carry a lower level of risk. They tend to be less volatile than other investments and provide a more consistent return on investment.

Bonds can contribute to the creation of a diversified portfolio, which can help to lower the overall risk associated with the portfolio. This is due to the fact that bonds, in general, do not have the same degree of correlation with other assets such as equities.

Preservation of capital: Bonds are a tool that can be utilized to assist in the preservation of capital, particularly during times of increased market volatility. This is due to the fact that at the time of the bond's maturity, the investor typically receives back the principal amount that was put in the bond.

The following are some of the risks connected with investing in bonds:

The risk posed by interest rates comes from the inverse relationship between bond prices and interest rates. When interest rates go up, the value of bonds that are already in existence goes down, and vice versa.

High-yield bonds, sometimes known as junk bonds, are a type of bond that has a greater credit risk than other types of bonds. These bonds can be issued by firms or governments. These bonds come with a higher risk of default, which means that an investor may end up losing the primary amount of money put in them.

The value of a bond's fixed interest payments may be reduced over time due to inflation, which is a risk that investors face.

The possibility exists that certain bonds will have a call clause, which grants the issuer the right to repurchase the bond prior to the date on which it is scheduled to mature. Because of this, the investor runs the risk of missing out on any future interest payments.

Adding funds to your portfolio is an excellent strategy to increase the diversity of your holdings and potentially increase your returns. A fund is a type of collective investment vehicle that pools the capital contributed by a number of different participants in order to make investments in a diverse range of assets, including stocks, bonds, and commodities. The following are some steps that will assist you in investing in a fund:

It is crucial to identify your financial goals before you invest in a fund. Before you do so, you should determine what your investment goals are. Do you want to have gains in the short term or returns in the long run? Investing for retirement? What other specific financial objective do you have in mind? If you are aware of your goals, selecting the type of fund that best meets your needs in terms of investments will be much easier.

Do some research on the various kinds of funds There are many different kinds of funds available, each with its own investment strategy and level of risk. Mutual funds, exchange-traded funds (ETFs), hedge funds, and index funds are some of the most prevalent kinds of funds. Hedge funds are also a sort of fund. Conduct research on the many kinds of funds available, and select the one that best meets your needs in terms of investments.

Choose a fund: After you have determined your investment objectives and been familiar with the various categories of funds, it is time to choose a particular fund to invest in. You should look for a fund that has a solid management team, affordable fees, and an excellent track record of performance in the past. You should read the prospectus for the fund since it contains in-depth information about the investment goals, strategy, and potential hazards of the fund.

You will need to open an investing account in order to invest in a fund; this account can be opened with a brokerage business or a financial institution. You have the option of opening an account in person or opening one online. Fidelity, Schwab, and Vanguard are just a few names that come to mind when discussing well-known brokerage businesses.

Investing in funds requires you to first open an investing account and then transfer money into that account so that it may be used to make investments. This can be accomplished by moving money from one of your bank accounts to another, or by depositing a check.

Put in your order: Once you've deposited money into your account, you'll be able to put in an order to acquire shares of the fund. You have the option of investing a single sum or setting up recurring investments with pre-determined amounts being contributed regularly.

After putting money into a fund, you should make it a habit to check in on your investment on a frequent basis to make sure it is still in line with the objectives you set for your portfolio. Review the performance of the fund and make any necessary adjustments to ensure that your investment portfolio stays on track.

Mutual Funds

A mutual fund is a sort of investment instrument that pools money from several investors in order to purchase securities such as stocks, bonds, or other assets. Mutual funds can also be used to invest in other types of assets. Professional fund managers are in charge of the selection and management of the investments held inside these funds. These managers are responsible for the overall management of the funds. Because they provide investors with a number of benefits, including diversification, expert management, and convenience, mutual funds are a common choice among individuals as an investment vehicle.

Investing in mutual funds offers diversification, which is one of the most significant benefits of doing so. Mutual funds are able to invest in a diverse range of securities because they pool their investors' funds with those of other investors, which helps to spread out risk. This indicates that if one investment performs poorly, it will be offset by the gains that are generated by the other assets that are contained inside the fund. As a consequence of this, investors have the opportunity to obtain a level of diversification that would be challenging for them to accomplish on their own.

One more advantage of mutual funds is that they are handled by experts in the financial industry. The research and selection of the assets held by the fund is the responsibility of the fund manager. This can help to ensure that the fund is invested in high-quality securities that are suitable for the fund's investment goals. In addition, it is the responsibility of the fund management to monitor the portfolio and make appropriate adjustments to it as necessary. Doing so can help to maximize returns while minimizing risk.

One practical method of investing is through the use of mutual funds. Investors can purchase shares of the fund through a broker or a financial advisor, which enables them to invest a very small amount of capital in a diverse portfolio of securities. In addition, mutual funds provide investors with liquidity, which indicates that it is simple for investors to purchase and sell shares of the fund on a daily basis. This is something that might be very helpful for investors who require immediate access to their money. When it comes to choosing between different mutual funds, there are a number of considerations that investors need to keep in mind. The purpose of the fund's investments is one of the most crucial considerations to make. Investors should select a fund that is consistent with the objectives they have set for their portfolio.

Exchange-Traded Funds (ETFs)
Exchange-Traded Funds, or ETFs for short, are a type of investment fund that, similar to individual stocks, may be bought and sold on stock exchanges. The performance of a particular index or group of assets, such as stocks,

bonds, commodities, or currencies, can be replicated through the use of exchange-traded funds (ETFs). ETFs are gaining popularity among investors because of the cheap fees they charge, the diversity they offer, and the adaptability they offer.

Similar to stocks, exchange-traded funds (ETFs) can be purchased and sold at any time during the trading day, and their prices move up and down depending on how well the assets they track perform. Because of this, exchange-traded funds (ETFs) are a highly liquid investment choice for investors because they can be bought and sold rapidly and easily.

The very modest fees charged by ETFs are one of the main reasons why they are becoming increasingly popular. ETFs often have lower expense ratios than mutual funds, which makes them an appealing choice for investors who are concerned about keeping their investment costs low. Moreover, several brokers make it possible to trade exchange-traded funds (ETFs) without paying any commissions, which cuts the costs associated with investing even further.

One more advantage of ETFs is the diversification they provide. Investors can acquire exposure to a wide variety of securities with a single investment by purchasing exchange-traded funds (ETFs), which track a particular index or group of assets. This can help to reduce risk and produce more consistent returns throughout the course of the investment's lifetime.

ETFs provide investors with additional freedom in terms of the investment strategies they might employ. Some exchange-traded funds are designed to replicate the performance of broad market indices, while others follow indices that concentrate on particular industries, geographic regions, or investment themes. For instance, investors have the option to put their money into exchange-traded funds (ETFs) that follow equities of companies involved in the healthcare industry, renewable energy, or emerging markets.

Investors need to be aware that exchange-traded funds (ETFs), despite the benefits they offer, do not come risk-free. ETFs, like any other type of investment, are susceptible to the market's volatility as well as variations in the assets that underpin them. In addition, certain exchange-traded funds may have more complicated investment methods, which call for a more in-depth comprehension of the underlying assets as well as the investing approach.

Exchange-Traded Funds (ETFs) provide investors with a flexible investing choice that is also low cost and diversified. Because there is such a wide variety of ETFs to choose from, investors are able to craft investment strategies that are uniquely suited to fit their own objectives and comfort levels with risk. Before putting money into exchange-traded funds (ETFs), you must, as is the case with any other type of investment, give careful consideration to the potential downsides as well as upsides.

Investment in Real Estate Many people all over the world choose to put their money into real estate as an investment option. Numerous factors contribute to this phenomenon, including the fact that real estate is a tangible asset, the fact that it has the ability to generate consistent income, and the possibility that its value would rise over time. Nevertheless, investing in real estate calls for a significant amount of research and planning, in addition to careful evaluation of a wide range of aspects, including location, trends in the market, and the financial component of the transaction.

The possibility of a rise in value over a longer period of time is one of the most significant benefits associated with investing in real estate. As a result of population growth and the fact that real estate is a limited resource, there is a growing demand for property. This can result in an increase in property values over time, particularly in places that are desired to live in or in regions that are experiencing economic expansion. In addition, investments in real estate can generate passive income in the form of rental income from properties or profit from the sale of a property after its value has increased via appreciation.

The potential to leverage your investment is another another advantage that comes along with investing in real estate. When compared to other sorts of investments, such as stocks, bonds, or mutual funds, real estate can be purchased with a very little down payment, and the majority of the purchase price can be financed through a mortgage loan. This is in contrast to other types of investments, such as stocks, which require a substantial initial investment. This enables investors to use the money of other people to purchase property, which can result in a greater potential return on investment for the investor.

However, investing in real estate is not without its share of potential hazards. The value of real estate may fall as a consequence of economic downturns, excess construction in particular regions, or alterations in market demand. In addition, investments in real estate require constant management and maintenance, both of which can consume a lot of your time and money respectively. Investors need to be ready to deal with unforeseen costs, such as repairs or vacancies, which can have an influence on their cash flow. This includes being prepared to cope with unexpected expenses.

When contemplating making an investment in real estate, it is essential to carry out extensive research on the local market. This research should take into account a variety of criteria, including vacancy rates, rental prices, and economic trends. It is also essential to have a solid understanding of the investment's financial components, such as the potential for cash flow, the consequences for taxes, and the financing choices.

Commodities

Commodities Investment Guide

Physical things that are bought and sold in different markets around the world are known as commodities. They include agricultural items such as wheat, corn, and soybeans, as well as industrial metals such as copper, aluminum, and zinc. Raw materials such as crude oil, gold, and silver are also included in this category. Commodities play a key role in the operation of economies all over the world and are fundamental components of a wide variety of manufacturing processes.

Those investors looking to diversify their holdings and hedge themselves against the effects of inflation may find that investing in commodities presents them with a compelling opportunity. The fact that commodities have historically exhibited a low correlation with other asset classes such as stocks and bonds indicates that including commodities in a portfolio has the potential to both reduce overall portfolio volatility and boost returns.

Investing in commodities can be done in a variety of ways, including the following:

Investors have the ability to directly own and store commodities like as gold, silver, and other precious metals, as well as agricultural items such as wheat, soybeans, and maize. This type of ownership is referred to as "physical ownership."

Futures Contracts: Investors have the option to acquire futures contracts, which bind them to either buy or sell a certain commodity at a specified price and date in the future. Futures contracts can be purchased.

It is possible to lose money while investing in commodities due to the fact that the values of commodities can be unpredictable and are influenced by a wide variety of factors, including supply and demand, geopolitical events, and weather patterns. Investing in physical commodities also comes with the possibility of incurring charges for storage and insurance, and futures contracts call for a certain level of knowledge and skill.

Those investors who want to hedge their bets against inflation while also diversifying their portfolios might want to consider the possibility of investing in commodities. However, it is essential to maintain a prudent mindset when investing in commodities and to conduct exhaustive study before to making any decisions regarding investments.

Raw materials or finished goods that are traded on markets are both examples of commodities. Some common types of commodities are oil, gold, and wheat, amongst others. Investing in commodities may provide investors with the opportunity to diversify their portfolios and hedge against inflation; nevertheless, commodity investments are notorious for their high levels of volatility and susceptibility to shifts in supply and demand.

Cryptocurrencies

In recent years, investing in cryptocurrencies has become one of the most popular topics of conversation regarding potential investment prospects. In 2009, the world's first decentralized cryptocurrency, Bitcoin, was founded. Since that time, thousands upon thousands of different cryptocurrencies have been produced. Cryptocurrencies provide investors with a one-of-a-kind opportunity to invest in a digital currency that is decentralized and functions independently of governments and central banks through the use of blockchain technology.

The high degree of volatility that has historically been associated with cryptocurrencies such as Bitcoin has caused many potential investors to be wary of the asset class. Nevertheless, despite the high degree of volatility, cryptocurrency investments have produced some of the highest returns on investment over the past few years. Investing in cryptocurrency has helped some individuals amass fortunes worth millions and even billions of dollars.

The decentralized nature of cryptocurrency markets is one of the most attractive features of this asset class for investors. Cryptocurrencies, on the other hand, are not subject to the same regulations and constraints as traditional currencies are. Traditional currencies are controlled by governments and central banks, whereas cryptocurrencies are not. As a result, they are less prone to manipulation and inflation, which, over the long run, can make them a more reliable investment alternative.

One more benefit of utilizing cryptocurrency is the possibility of retaining one's anonymity. Because the transactions are recorded on a public blockchain ledger, there is a certain level of openness that assures the integrity of the transactions. This level of transparency also ensures that the transactions cannot be altered. On the other hand, the identity of the people involved in the transactions may be concealed, which may make it more challenging for governments or other bodies to monitor and control them.

Having said that, it is important to note that investing in cryptocurrencies is not without danger. If the market takes a turn for the worst, the high volatility of cryptocurrencies might result in huge losses for investors. In addition, because there is a lack of regulation and control in the cryptocurrency market, there is a possibility of fraud and frauds occurring within the market.

In spite of these dangers, investing in cryptocurrencies can still be a potentially successful venture for people who are prepared to do their research, invest properly, and monitor their returns. Investors have a responsibility to investigate and get an understanding of the underlying technologies of the cryptocurrencies in which they are investing, as well as the market patterns and potential hazards associated with the investments.

Those who are willing to assume the associated risks may find investing in cryptocurrencies to be an intriguing prospect. Because of the decentralized structure of cryptocurrencies and the fact that users can choose to remain anonymous when transacting with them, they present a novel investment opportunity that is exempt from the rules and restrictions that apply to conventional currencies.

Investors can choose from a wide variety of different types of investments, each of which comes with its own set of features, as well as advantages and disadvantages. Prior to making any decisions on investments, it is critical to give careful consideration to your long-term investment horizon, your risk tolerance, and any financial goals you have. Talking things over with a professional financial advisor can also help you make educated choices about how and where to invest your money in order to meet your various financial goals.

Diversification of investments is an essential tactic for women who desire to amass wealth and establish themselves as financially independent individuals. The practice of spreading one's investments among a number of distinct asset classes and securities in order to lower one's exposure to financial loss and increase one's potential for financial gain is known as diversification. When it comes to investing, you, as a woman, have particular hurdles, some of which include the gender pay gap, employment interruptions owing to caregiving commitments, and a higher life expectancy than males do. As a result, it is vital to choose a diversified investment plan that is appropriate for your goals, level of risk tolerance, and current financial status.

When building a diversified investing portfolio as a woman, the following are some important considerations to keep in mind:

The term "asset allocation" refers to the process of separating your investment portfolio into several asset classes such as stocks, bonds, real estate, and commodities. You can lessen the effect that market volatility has on your total results by diversifying your portfolio over a variety of asset classes. Each asset class has its own distinct risk and return profile. For instance, if the stock market is falling, the performance of your bond holdings may improve, so offsetting the losses that have occurred in your stock holdings.

Geographic diversification: To limit the risk of political and economic events that could have an effect on a particular market, it is essential to spread your investments over a number of countries and regions. Investing in foreign equities, bonds, and funds can also provide exposure to a variety of currencies and exchange rates, which can help minimize the impact that currency swings have on your portfolio.

Diversification of industries: Investing in a variety of businesses can assist lessen the risk of incurring losses in the event that one of an investor's target markets sees a decline. If you invest solely in technology companies, for instance, you run the risk of incurring big losses if the technology industry undergoes a recession. It is possible to lessen the effect that market volatility has on your investments by diversifying your investment portfolio across a number of different businesses.

CHAPTER 4

The investor's comfort level with risk

Investing is a strong tool that can be used to develop money and ensure a secure and comfortable future for oneself, but it does involve taking on some level of risk. A person's risk tolerance can be defined as the extent to which they are willing to expose themselves to potential losses in order to achieve prospective profits. Because women experience distinct financial issues and factors that can effect their investing strategy, it is especially important for women to understand and manage their risk tolerance. This is because women confront unique financial challenges and concerns.

Disparities in wealth and income based on gender

Women confront a number of gender-based financial inequities, all of which can have an effect on the investing choices they make. For instance, on average, women earn less money than males do, and they are more likely to take time off from work in order to care for their children or elderly relatives. This can result in decreased lifetime earnings, less benefits from Social Security, and an increased likelihood of living in poverty during retirement.

In addition, women typically live longer than males, which means that they need to set aside a greater amount of money for retirement in order to ensure that they have sufficient funds to endure for the entirety of their lives. On the other hand, women often have a smaller nest egg saved for retirement than men do, and they may also face higher healthcare costs during retirement as a result of longer life expectancies and larger healthcare requirements.

When it comes to investing, each of these elements has the potential to influence a woman's level of comfort with taking risks. For instance, if you are concerned about not having enough money for retirement, it is possible that you will be less willing to take risks and will choose assets that are safer. On the other hand, if you are not bothered by the prospect of taking on additional risk, you may be able to generate larger returns, which will allow you to make up for lost time when it comes to saving for retirement.

Aspects in one's life that can change their risk tolerance

When it comes to investments, your level of comfort with risk can be affected by a number of things, including the following:

Time horizon: In general, you will be able to take on a greater amount of risk if you have a longer time horizon for your investments. If you are investing for a goal that will be accomplished within the next several years, such as purchasing a home, you should probably stick to safer investments. On the other hand, if you are investing for a goal that is further in the future, such as retirement, you might be able to tolerate a higher level of risk.

Your current financial condition has the potential to influence the amount of risk you are willing to take. If you are struggling to make ends meet and have a high-paying job in addition to a sizable emergency fund, you may have less anxiety about taking risks than if you have both of these things.

Your risk tolerance might be affected, among other ways, by the goals you have set for your investments. When your objective is to maintain your current level of money, you might be less willing to take risks than when your objective is to increase your current level of wealth.

Personality is another factor that can have an effect on the amount of risk you are willing to take. If you have a low tolerance for risk by nature, you could feel more at ease with investments that are less hazardous. On the other side, if you find enjoyment in taking risks, you might feel more at ease with assets that are more volatile.

Taking risk management seriously as a female investor

When it comes to generating and protecting wealth as an investor, one of the most crucial aspects is risk management. The following is a list of risk management tactics that you can employ:

The practice of diversifying one's investing portfolio is widely recognized as one of the most effective strategies for risk management. This entails investing in a variety of asset types, such as stocks, bonds, and real estate, as well as diversifying your holdings across a variety of business sectors and geographic regions. Your exposure to the risk of loss from any one investment or industry can be reduced by diversification.

The term "asset allocation" refers to the division of your overall portfolio into the various asset classes to which you commit a certain percentage of its total value. Your financial goals, your time horizon, and your level of comfort with risk should all play a role in determining how you should allocate your assets. For instance, if you have a long investing horizon and are not bothered by the possibility of loss and are okay with risk, you might want to invest a bigger amount of your portfolio in equities.

The term "rebalancing" refers to the process of making periodic changes to your investment portfolio in order to keep it at the correct asset allocation. You may need to sell some stocks and purchase more bonds in order to rebalance your portfolio. For instance, if stocks have done well and now represent a bigger percentage of your portfolio than you expected, you may need to sell some stocks and buy more bonds.

The function that is played by financial advisors Investing may be an important element in the process of establishing long-term financial security, and working with a financial advisor can be a key component in ensuring that your investment selections are well-informed. It's possible that reaching your financial goals as a woman will present its own set of specific hurdles, such as the gender pay gap, taking time away from the workforce to care for family members, and living longer than men on average. Working with a financial advisor can be of great assistance to you in navigating these issues and developing a customized investment strategy that is in line with your objectives and priorities.

The following is a list of some of the ways that financial advisors can help you in your road of investment:

Putting together a customized investment strategy A financial advisor can work with you to establish a personalized investment strategy that takes into account your current financial circumstances, your long-term goals, and the amount of risk you are willing to take. They are able to assist you in determining the many kinds of investments that are appropriate for you, such as equities, bonds, mutual funds, or exchange-traded funds (ETFs), for example. They may also assist you in understanding the potential risks and benefits associated with the various investment options available to you and in the development of a diversified investment portfolio that is in line with your goals.

Investment is a long-term commitment, and financial advisers can provide continuous counsel and support to help you remain on track. Investing requires a long-term commitment, and financial advisors can help you stay on track by providing ongoing guidance and support. They can assist you in modifying your investment strategy to account for changes in your financial circumstances or goals, monitor the performance of your investments, and offer guidance regarding the appropriate times to buy, sell, or hold investments.

Providing you with education on various investment techniques A reliable financial advisor can assist you in comprehending the fundamentals of investing as well as a variety of investment strategies. They can simplify difficult financial concepts for you and assist you in making educated decisions depending on your comfort level with risk and the goals you wish to achieve with your investments. It is of the utmost importance for you, as a woman, to collaborate with a financial advisor who is well-informed about the specific issues you may experience as a result of your gender when it comes to investing and who is able to provide advice that is suited to your individual requirements.

Emotional assistance: Because investing can be an emotionally taxing process, working with a financial advisor can give you with the necessary emotional support to help you maintain your course. They can assist you in avoiding common hazards associated with investing, such as selling stocks during bear markets or investing an excessive amount of money in a single asset. In addition, they can act as a sounding board for your investing ideas and assist you in maintaining your discipline despite the volatility of the market.

When it comes to reaching your long-term financial goals, having the assistance of a financial advisor might be an essential step. A qualified financial advisor will be able to assist you in developing a customized investment strategy, offer continuous direction and support, educate you about investment methods, and provide emotional support as needed.

CHAPTER 5

Retirement planning

Planning for retirement is an essential step in effectively managing your finances and getting ready for a future that is both pleasant and safe. It entails establishing financial goals, determining an estimate of the costs associated with retirement, and devising a savings plan to meet those objectives. It is critical to make enough preparations for retirement since doing so enables you to preserve your current standard of life, enjoy your senior years, and reach a level of financial independence.

The first thing you should do when preparing your retirement is to figure out what you want your retirement to look like. You need to give some thought to the kind of lifestyle you wish to maintain during your retirement years and calculate the amount of money that will be required to fund that lifestyle. Your current age, your anticipated retirement age, your life expectancy, and your current state of health are all factors that can have an impact on your retirement aspirations.

After you have decided what you want to do, the following step is to calculate how much money you will need for retirement. You need to take into account all of your expenses, including those that are required and those that are optional, such as accommodation, food, medical care, transportation, and entertainment. When calculating an estimate of your costs, it is vital to take inflation into account because, as a general rule, the cost of living will go up over time.

You will be able to assess how much money you need to save in order to reach your objectives after you have estimated the costs associated with your retirement. You need to give some thought to the various options available to you for generating income during retirement, such as Social Security benefits, pensions, and personal savings. You may also want to give some thought to the possibility of generating money during retirement through activities such as making investments in real estate or working part-time while retired.

Putting together a savings strategy for retirement is one of the most important things you can do to ensure you meet your retirement objectives. You need to give some thought to the many possibilities available to you in terms of retirement savings, including 401(k)s, individual retirement accounts (IRAs), and taxable investment accounts. You should also evaluate the level of risk that you are willing to accept with your investments. Riskier investments have the potential to produce bigger returns, but they also come with higher levels of danger. You should think carefully about the level of risk that you are willing to take with your investments.

It is crucial to routinely assess and make any necessary adjustments to your plan for saving for retirement. Because your current financial condition and your plans for retirement could shift over time, it is essential to monitor and adjust your savings strategy accordingly. It's possible that in order to keep your financial stability, you'll need to make some changes to the amount of money you save each month, the way you invest your money, or your plans for retirement.

It is essential to plan not just for one's retirement savings but also for other areas of retirement, such as one's healthcare and estate affairs, in addition to saving for retirement. During retirement, the cost of medical care can become a substantial burden, which is why it is important to take into consideration aspects such as Medicare coverage and long-term care insurance. Additionally, estate planning can help guarantee that your assets are dispersed in accordance with your preferences and can limit the tax liabilities that your heirs will be responsible for after your death.

The process of planning for retirement is an important one that needs to be approached with caution and involves much preparation. You can achieve financial security and have a nice retirement by planning out your retirement goals, calculating how much money you will need in retirement, and implementing a savings plan. You can assist ensure that you stay on pace to reach your goals and retain financial independence throughout your golden years by regularly assessing and modifying as necessary any changes you make to your retirement plan.

A Comprehensive Look at Retirement Accounts

It is crucial to take into consideration the many forms of retirement accounts that are obtainable when one is making preparations for retirement. Individuals are given the opportunity to save for their retirement in a manner that is advantageous from a tax point of view through the use of retirement accounts. There are numerous options for saving for retirement, such as 401(k) plans, individual retirement accounts (IRAs), and pensions.

401(k) Plans

One variety of retirement plan is known as a 401(k) plan, and it is one that is sponsored by an employer. It gives employees the opportunity to make pre-tax contributions to their retirement accounts, which then have the potential to grow tax-free until the time when the funds are withdrawn during retirement. A matching contribution is something that some firms offer to their employees, which can help them save even more money for their retirement.

Contributions to a 401(k) plan are normally capped at a particular percentage of an employee's annual pay, and the Internal Revenue Service (IRS) imposes a cap on the total amount that can be contributed to such plans. Those who are over the age of 50 are eligible to make an additional catch-up contribution of $6,500 to their 401(k) plan in 2021. The maximum contribution limit for a 401(k) plan is $19,500 in 2021.

One of the benefits of participating in a 401(k) plan is the ability to have pre-tax dollars deducted from one's paycheck on a pre-determined schedule. This makes it much simpler to set money aside for one's retirement. In addition, many businesses provide their workers with a selection of investment choices within the plan, enabling workers to select assets that are suitable for their level of comfort with risk as well as their ambitions for their retirement.

Accounts for Individual Retirement (also known as IRAs) A retirement savings account that is not associated with a specific company is known as an Individual Retirement Account, or IRA for short. The most common kinds of Individual Retirement Accounts (IRAs) are known as standard and Roth IRAs.

Traditional Individual Retirement Accounts (IRAs) enable individuals to make contributions before taxes, which can then grow free of taxation until the funds are taken after retirement. It is possible for an individual's contributions to a typical Individual Retirement Account (IRA) to qualify for a tax deduction based on the individual's income as well as other circumstances. Withdrawals made from a typical individual retirement account (IRA) are taxed in the same manner as other types of income.

On the other hand, individuals are able to make contributions to their Roth IRAs after they have already paid their taxes. Despite the fact that contributions to a Roth IRA do not qualify for a tax deduction, earnings that accumulate on those contributions do not incur taxation, and qualifying withdrawals from a Roth IRA are also not subject to taxation. Because of the increased leeway provided by Roth IRAs regarding the timing of contribution withdrawals, these accounts are becoming an increasingly popular choice among investors.

The maximum amount that can be contributed to a regular or Roth IRA in 2021 is $6 000. Individuals who are over the age of 50 are eligible for a catch-up contribution of an additional $1 000.

Pensions A pension is a type of retirement plan that is often made available by employers in particular fields, such as the public sector and the educational system. Pensions are intended to provide a reliable source of income for retirees, and the amount of money that retirees get from their pensions is based on a variety of criteria, including the employee's average yearly wage and length of service.

When an employee has a pension, the employee's employer is the one who is responsible for managing the investments and making payments into the plan. Depending on the particular design of the plan, it's possible that employees will be expected to make payments to the plan as well. Pensions are typically financed by a contribution from both the employee and the employer, in addition to gains from investments.

One of the benefits of a pension is that it ensures a steady stream of income during retirement, which can provide retirees a sense of security and help them enjoy their golden years. However, not all workers are eligible for pensions, and the amount of the pension payout may be subject to shifts depending on the conditions of the market and other aspects of the worker's situation.

There are several distinct options available for retirement accounts, and each one comes with its own set of benefits as well as potential drawbacks. When deciding which sort of retirement account to use, it is critical to take into account both your individual plans for retirement and your current financial circumstances. Talking things over with a trusted financial professional before settling on a plan for your retirement savings can also help you make more educated choices.

Maximizing Retirement Savings.
The decision to retire is a significant life milestone that calls for extensive preparation and meticulous planning. Putting away enough money so that you won't need to depend on Social Security or any other form of assistance once you stop working is one of the most essential steps in getting ready for retirement. Sadly, a lot of people don't start thinking about their retirement savings until it's already too late to do something about it. Because of this, it is extremely important to get a head start on planning for retirement as soon as you possibly can and to implement a variety of tactics to ensure that your retirement resources are maximized.

Taking advantage of company matching programs is one of the most effective strategies to boost the amount of retirement savings you have accumulated. Many firms provide matching contributions to the retirement accounts of their employees. This means that the company will contribute an amount equal to or greater than a predetermined percentage of the employee's total contributions, up to a predetermined maximum. For instance, a company might offer to contribute an additional 6% of the employee's salary in addition to matching 50% of the employee's contributions. You can effectively double the amount of money you have saved for retirement with no more work on your part if you make sufficient contributions to qualify for the matching program.

Taking advantage of catch-up contributions is yet another approach you may implement to get the most out of your retirement funds. Individuals over the age of 50 are eligible to make catch-up payments, which enable them to deposit additional funds to their retirement accounts on an annual basis. For 401(k) plans, the catch-up contribution maximum is now set at $6,500 for the year 2021. This is in addition to the regular contribution limit, which is currently set at $19,500. Contributions made during the catch-up period might be especially beneficial for those who have not set aside enough money for retirement or who are trying to make up for lost time.

It is essential to invest your funds for retirement in a way that minimizes the impact of taxes, in addition to participating in employer-sponsored retirement savings programs and making catch-up payments if eligible. Because of this, you may be able to maximize your savings while also decreasing your tax liability. Investing in tax-advantaged retirement accounts, such as 401(k) plans, traditional IRAs, or Roth IRAs, is one strategy for achieving this goal. These accounts give you access to a variety of tax benefits, such as growth that is exempt from taxation or withdrawals that are not subject to taxation, which can assist you in economizing more money over the course of a longer period of time.

Investing in low-cost index funds or exchange-traded funds (ETFs) is another method of investment that minimizes the impact of taxes. These investments are created to mimic the behavior of a certain market index, such as the S&P 500, and typically have lower fees and expenditures than actively managed funds due to their passive management style. Investing in index funds gives you the opportunity to possibly earn higher returns while allowing you to pay lesser fees, which can help you optimize the amount of money you save for retirement.

Your investment portfolio for retirement should be diversified by including holdings in a variety of asset classes, such as stocks, bonds, and other investment vehicles. You may be able to better control risk and, as a result, perhaps generate higher profits over the long run as a result of this. However, it is essential to keep in mind that diversity does not ensure a profit or guard against loss. You should speak with a financial counselor in order to find the proper investment mix for your unique requirements and objectives.

Increasing the amount of money you have saved for retirement can be accomplished in a number of ways. Some of these methods include participating in employer matching programs, making catch-up payments, and investing in a tax-efficient manner. You might potentially save enough money to support yourself during your retirement years if you start using these tactics at an early stage and invest in a broad portfolio of assets. It is never too early to start planning for retirement, so don't be afraid to start examining your alternatives and building a plan that is tailored to your specific needs as soon as possible.

CHAPTER 6

Debt Management Strategies

Keeping track of all of your financial obligations can be a difficult and frustrating process, especially if you have a lot of different bills or a large total amount of debt. However, it is possible to regain control of your debt and attain financial stability if you approach the situation with thorough planning and a disciplined attitude. In this piece, we will go over a few different methods that can help you efficiently manage your debt.

Establish a spending plan.
The creation of a budget is the initial stage in the process of debt management. Creating a budget will enable you to keep track of both your income and your costs, as well as locate areas in which you can reduce your spending. You will be able to track where your money is going and make

modifications to pay off debt more quickly if you create a budget so that you can keep track of it.

Prioritize your debts

After you have constructed a budget, the next step is to arrange your debts in descending order of importance. Create a list of all of your obligations, including the rates of interest and the minimum payments required for each one. Make a list of your debts in order of highest interest rate, with the debt that has the highest interest rate at the very top of the list. This will make it easier for you to concentrate your efforts on clearing the debts that are accruing the greatest interest charges for you.

Discuss terms with your creditors.

If you are having trouble making your payments on your debt, you may want to discuss the possibility of bargaining with your creditors. It's possible that you'll be able to negotiate a reduced interest rate or a payment schedule that's more workable given the constraints of your financial situation. It is essential to communicate openly and honestly with your creditors regarding the state of your finances at all times and to keep them abreast of your progress.

Consider debt consolidation

Consolidating your many loans into a single loan with a reduced interest rate is an option to explore if you have a number of different obligations with varying interest rates. Your monthly payments can be made more manageable and you could end up paying less interest overall if you consolidate your debt. When contemplating the option of consolidating debt, it is essential to exercise caution and check that the new loan features a reduced interest rate and is within the scope of your financial capabilities.

Boost the amount of money you make.

Increasing your income is one strategy you can employ to reduce your debt more quickly. You can accomplish this goal by working an additional job, engaging in freelance work, or selling things that you no longer use. If you increase your income, you will have more money available for the repayment of your debts, which will enable you to pay off your obligations sooner.

Avoid additional debt

It is imperative that you refrain from accruing any additional debt while you are working toward paying off the debt you already have. This entails abstaining from making purchases with credit cards and other forms of debt. If you must make a purchase, give preference to paying for it with cash or a debit card if at all possible.

Seek the assistance of professionals.
If you are having trouble keeping track of your debt, you may want to consider getting assistance from a professional. You may benefit from working with a credit counselor or financial advisor who can assist you in developing a plan for managing your debt and offer advice on how to handle your finances. In addition to this, they are able to assist you in negotiating with your creditors and provide resources for debt consolidation and other methods of debt management.

The process of managing debt might be a difficult one, but it is doable with the application of rigorous planning and self-discipline. You can gain control of your debt and attain financial stability if you establish a budget, assign priorities to your bills, negotiate with your creditors, consider consolidating your debt, increase the amount of money you bring in each month, refrain from taking on any new debt, and seek expert assistance.

A financial commitment or liability that is due by one party to another is referred to as debt. The term "debt" refers to a variety of financial obligations that can be incurred for a wide range of purposes, including the financing of a business venture, the acquisition of a residence or vehicle, or the payment of educational expenses. In the following paragraphs, we will discuss several distinct kinds of debt, such as credit card debt, student loans, and mortgages.

Credit Card Debt
One of the most popular kinds of debt today is that which is carried on credit cards. It is a form of unsecured debt, which means that it is not supported by collateral such as a house or a car in the event that the borrower defaults on the loan. When you use a credit card to pay for something, you are essentially taking out a loan from the company that issued the credit card. If you do not pay off the balance in full by the due date, you will be subject to interest charges on the sum that is still outstanding.

Credit card debt can be problematic due to the high interest rates that are often associated with it. These rates can quickly build up if you continue to carry a load from one month to the next. In addition, spontaneous purchases and spending more money than one has available are frequently the causes of credit card debt. It is imperative that credit cards be used in a responsible manner and that the full balance be paid off each month, if at all feasible, in order to prevent going into credit card debt.

Student Loans

Student loans are a form of debt that can be used to pay for a variety of education-related expenses, including school fees, textbooks, and tuition. The most common kinds of student loans are classified as either federal or private. The federal government is the entity that is responsible for issuing student loans, and these loans, in comparison to private loans, often have interest rates that are lower and more flexible repayment alternatives. On the other side, financial institutions such as banks, credit unions, and other types of financial organizations are the ones that provide private student loans.

The enormous amount of debt that many students rack up is one of the most difficult aspects of taking out student loans to pay for their education. The entire outstanding balance of student loans in the United States is estimated to be more than $1.7 trillion, as reported by the Federal Reserve. Graduates who are just starting their professions and may not yet have the money necessary to make significant monthly payments on their debt may find it especially difficult to manage the financial load of this obligation.

Mortgages

A mortgage is a specific kind of debt that is taken out in order to buy a house. Mortgages, just like student loans, can come from the government or from a private lender. The Federal Housing Administration (FHA) and the Department of Veterans Affairs (VA) are two of the government departments that are responsible for the distribution of federal mortgages. Banks, credit unions, and other types of financial institutions are the ones that are able to provide private mortgages.

One of the advantages of obtaining a mortgage is that it makes it possible for consumers to buy a property without first having to save up enough money to pay for it in full.

Debt Payoff Strategies

In today's culture, a significant amount of people struggle with the burden of excessive debt. Dealing with any kind of debt, whether it's from a credit card, a student loan, or any other type, can be extremely intimidating and stressful. You can, however, pay off your debt and take control of your money by employing one of the options that are available to you. The debt snowball and the debt avalanche are two common strategies for eliminating debt, and we're going to take a look at both of them in this post.

Method of Snowballing Debt

Paying off your obligations in the order of their smallest balances to their greatest balances is the basis of the popular debt repayment approach known as the debt snowball method. The following is a rundown of the many stages involved in the debt snowball method:

First, you will need to compile a list of all of your obligations, in order from least to highest balance.

Step 2: Make the required minimum payments on all of your debts, with the exception of the one that is the least significant.

Step 3: If you have any spare money at the end of each month, put it toward paying down the loan with the least balance.

Step 4: Once you have paid off the loan with the shortest balance, take the money you were putting toward that obligation and put it toward the debt with the next smallest balance on your list.

Step 5: Continue doing this method until all of your financial obligations have been satisfied.

The debt snowball method is efficient mainly due to the fact that it offers a feeling of fulfillment quite early on in the process. When you pay off the loan with the smallest balance first, you get a fast win and a sense of momentum, both of which can drive you to keep working toward paying off the rest of your debt.

Debt Avalanche Method

Another common approach to paying off debt is known as the debt avalanche method, which requires working backwards from the loan with the highest interest rate to the debt with the lowest interest rate. The following is a rundown of the several stages involved in the debt avalanche method:

First, you will need to compile a list of all of your obligations, in order of greatest interest rate to lowest.

Step 2: Make sure you are paying at least the minimum amount due on all of your bills, with the exception of the debt that has the highest interest rate.

Step 3: Direct any additional funds you have each month toward eliminating the debt that is charging you the highest rate of interest.

Step Four: Once the debt with the highest interest rate has been paid off, take the money you were putting towards it and apply it to the debt on your list that has the next highest interest rate.

Step 5: Continue doing this method until all of your financial obligations have been satisfied.

The debt avalanche strategy is efficient because, over the course of time, it helps you save the most money possible on interest payments. If you pay off your debts with the highest interest rates first, you will lower the total amount of interest you will have to pay over the course of time, which will save you a significant amount of money if you do this in the right order.

Which Approach Is the Best Fit for You?

The debt snowball method and the debt avalanche method are two successful approaches to the problem of paying off debt. However, the approach that is ideal for you will be determined by the specifics of your situation. When determining which approach to use, there are a few things to keep in mind, including the following:

Your Personality: If you are someone who needs to see rapid gains in order to maintain their motivation, the debt snowball method may be the ideal option for you. The debt avalanche strategy is one that can be more suitable for you if you are more concerned with long-term savings.

Your Debt: The debt snowball strategy is likely to be more successful for you if you have a number of smaller obligations with comparable interest rates. It's possible that the debt avalanche strategy will work better for you if you have high-interest bills.

If you have a limited cash flow and need to free up some money in the short term, the debt snowball method may be the ideal option for you to use to pay off your debts. The debt avalanche strategy may be more suitable for your situation if you have a greater ability to generate cash flow and are financially able to make larger payments.

No matter which strategy you decide to implement, the most essential thing is to get a head start on paying off your debt as quickly as you possibly can. The debt snowball approach and the debt avalanche method are both great tactics for paying off debt; thus, choose the method that works best for your circumstances and get started working toward a life free of financial obligations.

Building a Financial Team

Building your financial team is a critical step toward securing your financial future as a woman, and you should take this step right away. You may improve your ability to make educated decisions and move closer toward achieving your financial goals by assembling a group of experts who can assist you with various elements of your finances.

As a woman, here are some suggestions that can assist you in building your financial team:

Determine Your Needs The first thing you need to do in order to construct a successful financial team is to determine your needs. Consider which aspects of your financial life, such as investing, tax preparation, retirement planning, or estate planning, you require assistance with and think about how you may get it. Taking this into consideration will assist you in identifying which professionals are required for your team.

do Research and Make a Selection of specialists Once you have determined your requirements, the next step is to do research and make a selection of the financial specialists who can assist you in achieving your objectives. Look for specialists who have a track record of successfully collaborating with female clients and who have a solid standing in the industry. A financial planner, an accountant, an attorney, and an insurance agent are all examples of professionals that you can find useful to have on your team.

Establish a Relationship: Establishing a rapport with the members of your financial team is of the utmost importance. Set up regular meetings to go through your finances and talk about your accomplishments, goals, and any problems you have. Be certain that the members of your team comprehend both your aims and your values, and that they are trying to realize the former.

Choosing to Comprise Your Financial Team With Women Professionals It may be to your advantage to compile your financial team with women professionals. Because women are typically more empathic, communicative, and collaborative than men, you could feel more at ease talking to a female financial advisor about your issues and ambitions in this area. In addition, women professionals may have more expertise working with the particular requirements and difficulties that women face in the financial sphere.

It is important that you communicate your priorities to others because, when it comes to money, you may have different priorities than males. Share with your financial team the things that are most important to you, such as maintaining a healthy work-life balance, beginning a family, or taking care of aging parents. This will allow them to better adapt their advise to your specific requirements and objectives.

Finally, it is vital to review your strategy on a regular basis in order to verify that you are on the right route to attaining your objectives in terms of your financial situation. Make any necessary adjustments, and ensure that your financial team is aware of any shifts in either your priorities or your current situation.

Putting together a financial support network as a woman is one of the most important steps you can take toward safeguarding your financial future. You may accomplish your financial goals and live the life you want to live if you first determine your needs, then choose the appropriate specialists, then create relationships, then pick women professionals, then communicate your priorities, and finally review your strategy on a regular basis.

Locating Competent Financial Professionals.

When it comes to the management of our finances, it is critical to have a group of seasoned specialists who are aligned with our monetary ideals and objectives. It is essential to locate a professional who can assist you in achieving your financial goals and who is familiar with your values and priorities, regardless of whether you are looking for a financial advisor, an accountant, an attorney, or another type of expert.

The following are some ways that can be used to locate professionals who share your financial beliefs and goals and to collaborate with them:

Identify Your Financial Values and Goals
The first thing you need to do in order to find financial professionals that match your values and objectives is to determine what those values and objectives are. Do you place a high value on putting money down for your retirement? Do you wish to make investments in funds that are socially responsible? Do you want to get out from under your debt or put money down for a down payment on a house?

If you are aware of the most important aspects of your financial situation, you will be better able to choose the kind of assistance and guidance you require from a financial professional. For instance, if you place a high value on socially responsible investment, you might want to look for a financial advisor who focuses on that particular field of expertise.

Ask for Referrals

Asking friends, family, and coworkers for referrals is one of the most effective ways to identify financial specialists that share your priorities and objectives with regard to your financial situation. If you know someone who has similar financial priorities as you do, you should inquire about the people they deal with and whether or not they are satisfied with the services they receive.

You can also try looking up reviews and testimonials about a specific professional on their website to get an idea of what other customers have to say about them.

Carry out the Interviews

It is crucial to conduct interviews before to hiring a professional in order to ensure that the person would be a good fit for your needs. You have the option to ask questions concerning their experience, the method that they use for financial planning, and the costs that they charge. It is also crucial to inquire as to whether or not they have expertise working with customers who have the same financial ideals and objectives as you do.

Pay close attention to the manner in which the expert speaks with you when you are going through the interview procedure. They appear to be paying attention to your issues and responding to your inquiries in a manner that is simple to grasp, right? Do they give the impression that they are truly interested in assisting you in achieving your financial goals?

Investigate Their Qualifications

It is essential to confirm that the specialists you will be working with have the appropriate certifications and licenses before entrusting them with your finances. For instance, individuals who provide financial advice ought to be registered either with the Securities and Exchange Commission (SEC) or with state regulators. Licenses to practice as Certified Public Accountants (CPA) are required for accountants.

Look up a professional's profile on the website of the SEC's Investment Adviser Public Disclosure (IAPD) or the website of the American Institute of Certified Public Accountants (AICPA) to verify their credentials.

Establishing Direct Communication is Essential.
It is essential to have open lines of communication after you have engaged the services of a professional. Be certain that they have an understanding of your monetary objectives and ambitions, and then request that they

clarify their recommendations and tactics in a manner that can be easily comprehended.

In addition to this, it is essential that you determine how you will communicate with one another. Are face-to-face gatherings going to be a regular occurrence? Will you interact via email or phone? Check that the frequency of the communication and the method of it don't bother you too much.

Conduct Frequent Audits of Your Plan.
Last but not least, a frequent evaluation of your financial plan is essential to ensuring that you are on the right path to accomplishing your objectives. Make sure to check in with your professional on a frequent basis so that they can monitor your progress and provide feedback on how you can improve.

If you follow these tactics, you will be able to locate and collaborate with professionals that have the same financial beliefs and objectives as you. If you have the appropriate people working for you, you can be assured that you are on the correct track to accomplishing your monetary goals.

CHAPTER 7

Strategies for the Protection of Assets

To preserve your financial security and stability, one of the most crucial steps you can take is to protect your possessions. Your assets could include things like your home, automobile, investments, savings, business, and several other important goods and holdings. Whether you are just starting to create your wealth or have already amassed a substantial number of assets, it is vital to take steps to safeguard them from potential risks and threats. This is true whether you are just starting to build your wealth or have already accumulated a large amount of assets.

Obtain proper insurance coverage: Acquiring sufficient insurance coverage is one of the most fundamental and fundamental steps you can take to protect your possessions. Insurance plans can lessen the financial toll that unexpected occurrences like natural disasters, accidents, theft, or legal action can take on its policyholders. You might want to look into purchasing several types of insurance, such as homeowner's insurance, auto insurance, life insurance, disability insurance, liability insurance, and so on, depending on your individual requirements and preferences.

Maintain good documentation: It is essential to the safety of your assets that you maintain a well-organized and up-to-date collection of financial and legal documents. Make sure that copies of crucial documents like your will, trust paperwork, property deeds, contracts, and insurance policies are kept in a location that is both safe and easy to access. You should also think about employing cloud-based platforms or digital storage solutions to protect your papers from being physically damaged or lost. These options are both available today.

Invest in a number of markets and assets to help spread your risk and lessen the possible impact of swings in the market. Diversifying your investments will help you with both of these goals. Rather than placing all of your eggs in one basket, you should think about diversifying your portfolio by investing in a variety of asset classes such as stocks, bonds, real estate, commodities, and other markets. You should also give some thought to consulting with a financial counselor or investment specialist to assist you in making educated decisions regarding your investments.

Reduce the amount of risk you expose yourself to by keeping your liabilities under control. Doing so will also help you safeguard your assets. Try to avoid taking on any additional debt that isn't absolutely essential, and make it a priority to pay off any loans or credit card bills that you currently have. If you are the owner of a business, you may want to consider forming the company as a limited liability company (LLC) or a corporation so that you may keep your personal assets distinct from your business obligations.

Prepare yourself for the unexpected Finally, one of the most important things to do is to be prepared for the unexpected and to have a backup plan ready to go. Having a trust or estate plan in place to ensure that your assets are distributed in accordance with your preferences, having a power of attorney or healthcare proxy in place in the event that you become incapacitated, and having an emergency fund to cover unanticipated bills or loss of income are all examples of this type of preparation.

Taking preventative actions, carefully preparing your defenses, and maintaining constant vigilance are all essential components of an effective asset protection strategy. If you follow these tactics, you may reduce the amount of risk to your financial situation and protect your wealth for yourself and the people you care about. Don't forget to revisit your asset protection strategy on a regular basis and bring it up to date in order to maintain its applicability and efficiency in the face of shifting conditions.

Acquiring an Understanding of the Different Types of Insurance

Insurance is a form of risk management that can protect individuals, businesses, and even entire organizations against the financial fallout of unforeseen dangers or losses. There are many different kinds of insurance policies, and they cover a wide variety of life risks, including those related to one's health, life, property, and company. It is essential for individuals to have a thorough understanding of the many categories of insurance plans that are available in order to assist them in making educated judgments when picking an insurance policy. The following is a list of the various types of insurance policies:

Life Insurance

In the event of your passing, your loved ones can rely on the funds from your life insurance policy to help ease their financial burdens. The beneficiary receives a one-time payment in the case of the death of the policyholder. The policyholder is responsible for paying the premium. Life insurance is an essential tool for people who have dependents or who want to make certain that their loved ones will be financially secure in the event of their passing away. There are two primary classifications of life insurance policies: term life insurance and permanent life insurance.

Insurance for Medical Care

The financial burden of medical expenses, including as hospitalization, visits to the doctor, and the purchase of prescription drugs, might be shared among those with health insurance. It is possible for individuals to get it, or an organization may offer it to their employees as part of their benefits package. There is a wide range of variety in terms of coverage, premiums, and deductibles across health insurance policies.

Disability Insurance

Individuals who are unable to work as a result of an injury or illness and have purchased disability insurance are eligible to receive financial help from the policy. The policyholder will continue to receive a monthly payout equal to a percentage of their income until they are able to go back to work or achieve retirement age, whichever comes first.

Auto Insurance

The financial protection afforded by auto insurance can be utilized in the event of collisions involving motor vehicles such as cars, trucks, or motorcycles. Additionally, it might cover the policyholder's legal culpability for injuries or damage to property that they cause while driving. Different types of vehicles, coverage limits, and deductibles might result in vastly different insurance policies being purchased.

Insurance for Property Owners

Homeowners insurance offers monetary protection against monetary loss in the event of damage or loss to a home and its contents as a result of theft, fire, natural disasters, or any other incident that is covered by the policy. There is also the option to incorporate liability coverage in the policy for any incidents that take place on the property.

Business Insurance

Small, medium, and large enterprises alike can all benefit from the financial security that business insurance offers. It addresses a variety of concerns relating to a company, such as its property, liability, and workers' compensation needs. Insurance coverage for companies can be very different from one another depending on the type of company, the sector, and the particular risks involved.

Travel Insurance

In the event that a traveler is subjected to unforeseen circumstances while they are away from home, such as the cancellation of their trip, the loss of their luggage, or a medical emergency, travel insurance can protect them financially. It is also possible to cover things like trip cancellation, interruption, and delays with this plan.

Pet Insurance

Insurance for pets offers financial protection against the cost of veterinarian care and other types of medical treatment for animals. It may pay for treatment for illnesses, injuries, and even preventative care.

Insurance Against Flooding

Insurance against floods offers monetary protection against any losses incurred as a result of flooding. Standard homeowner's insurance policies do not cover damage caused by floods; thus, you will need to purchase special flood insurance.

Umbrella Insurance

Additional liability coverage over and above that which is provided by other insurance policies is made available through umbrella insurance. Its purpose is to safeguard private persons and commercial enterprises against the adverse monetary effects of legal actions and other unforeseen occurrences.

It is essential for individuals as well as organizations that want to protect themselves financially against unforeseen losses or hazards to have a solid understanding of the many types of insurance policies that are available. It is highly suggested to engage with an insurance agent or broker to choose the suitable insurance policy depending on the requirements of the individual or the business.

The prudent management of your assets should be a primary focus of your financial planning. Taking precautions to protect your assets can provide you peace of mind and help you ensure that your money will be passed down to next generations, regardless of whether you run a business, are an investor, or are simply an individual with a considerable amount of wealth.

The following is a list of various tactics that can be used to secure your assets:

Wills and estates planning: Wills and estates preparation is one of the most important things you can do to safeguard your assets. Putting together a detailed strategy for your assets that takes into account your goals, the requirements of your family, and the ramifications of the tax code is required. A will, a power of attorney, and a healthcare directive are the three components that should make up your estate plan.

A will is a legal document that states your wishes for the distribution of your possessions after your death. In the event that you are unable to make decisions involving your finances due to incapacity, a power of attorney can be used to appoint someone to make those decisions on your behalf. A healthcare directive can be used to specify your desires regarding medical treatment in the event that you are unable to make those decisions yourself.

Trusts are a type of legal structure in which one party (the trustee) is responsible for managing the assets of the trust on behalf of another party (the beneficiary). Trusts are an excellent tool for mitigating the effects of estate taxes, shielding assets from the claims of creditors, and ensuring that assets are dispersed in accordance with the terms of an individual's will.

There are numerous varieties of trusts, the most common of which are revocable trusts, followed by irrevocable trusts, and then asset protection trusts. When deciding on the kind of trust that's best for you, it's important to consult with an attorney who has plenty of knowledge in the field.

Insurance: Purchasing insurance can be an efficient strategy to safeguard your assets against the occurrence of unanticipated calamities. For instance, property and casualty insurance can cover your home and other belongings from being damaged or stolen in the event of an accident. You can be protected against lawsuits and other types of legal claims by purchasing liability insurance.

In addition to the standard insurance policies that are available, there are also specialized insurance products available, such as professional liability insurance and umbrella insurance, which can offer a higher level of protection.

Strategies for protecting one's assets Strategies for protecting one's assets comprise adopting preventative measures to safeguard one's assets from the claims of possible creditors. Creating an asset protection strategy via a limited liability company (LLC), establishing an offshore trust, or establishing a family limited partnership

(FLP) are all examples of conventional asset protection techniques.

By relocating assets to a country that has a more favorable legal system, offshore trusts are able to offer an additional layer of security to its beneficiaries. Because it enables you to transfer assets to a partnership that is subsequently managed by a member of your family or a trusted advisor, an FLP can provide you with protection for your assets.

Diversification: If you want to keep your investments safe, diversification is one of the most important strategies you can do. You can lessen the likelihood that a single occurrence or a decline in market conditions will cause you to lose all of your assets if you diversify your investments among a variety of asset classes, industries, and geographical locations.

A wide range of investment vehicles, such as index funds, exchange-traded funds (ETFs), and mutual funds, are all viable options for achieving diversification in one's portfolio.

Your assets should be protected at all times, which is an ongoing process that calls for careful planning and implementation. You will be able to establish a thorough strategy that takes into consideration your objectives, the risks involved, and the specifics of your situation if you work closely with an expert financial advisor and an attorney. You may ensure that your wealth will be passed down to subsequent generations by taking measures to secure your possessions and investments.

CHAPTER 8

Build a Legacy for yourself

It is not an easy effort to become a millionaire woman and build a legacy for oneself. It is necessary to have a clear vision, a dogged work ethic, and a dedication to have a beneficial effect on the world. On the other hand, the personal and professional benefits that come with leaving behind a lasting legacy are enormous. In this piece, we will discuss some of the most important things to keep in mind when planning your legacy as a millionaire woman.

Establishing Your mission and Values Establishing your mission and establishing your values is the first stage in constructing your legacy. What are some of the goals that you want to achieve in your life, and what are some of the values that are most important to you? Your sense of purpose and the values you hold dear will serve as a compass in everything you undertake, from the companies in which you invest to the charitable organizations you back.

Create a Powerful Network: If you want to leave a lasting impression, networking is essential. You have access to an enormous network of accomplished and prominent people thanks to the fact that you are a billionare lady. Make the most of this network's resources by cultivating fruitful partnerships with other business owners, investors, and influential thought leaders. Put yourself in the company of people who can support you in achieving your objectives and who share your perspective.

Invest in Your Business It is essential to invest in your business if you want to leave a prosperous legacy for future generations. You need to be willing to put in the effort, money, and other resources required to make your business a success, whether you are launching a brand-new enterprise or expanding an existing one. This requires being prepared to take measured risks while also being willing to invest in cutting-edge technologies and hire the greatest staff available.

Help Other Women Achieve Their Goals You, as a female billionaire, are in a unique position to assist other successful female entrepreneurs in achieving their goals. You have the ability to have a big impact on the lives of other women, whether it be through the act of mentoring, investing, or donating to organizations that promote women's concerns and causes in general. You are not only helping to develop your legacy when you support other women, but you are also laying the path for future generations of women who are interested in starting their own businesses.

Give Back to Your Community Building a lasting legacy requires that you play an active role in the betterment of the community in which you live. You have the ability to create a great influence in your town, whether it be through charity, volunteering, or supporting local companies. When you help other people out, not only are you making a positive change in their lives, but you are also leaving behind a legacy of kindness and charity for future generations.

Embrace innovation since it is the most important factor in creating a successful legacy. As a woman who is worth a billion dollars, you have to be prepared to accept new forms of communication, ideas, and ways of thinking. This entails maintaining an attitude that is receptive to novel possibilities and courageous enough to embrace potential downsides. You will not only be able to stay one step ahead of the competition if you are open to new ideas, but you will also leave a lasting legacy of development and expansion.

Pay Attention to Sustainability: If you want to leave a long-lasting legacy, you need to pay attention to sustainability. You have a responsibility, as a woman who is worth a billion dollars, to ensure that the ways in which you do business are both environmentally sustainable and socially responsible. This necessitates making investments in renewable forms of energy, cutting down on waste, and promoting ethical labor practices. You will leave a legacy of ethical business practices in addition to a better planet for future generations if you center your efforts on sustainability. This will allow you to pass on your values to the next generation.

It takes a strong sense of purpose, a commitment to hard work, and a willingness to take risks in order to build your legacy as a billionare woman. You may leave a legacy that will live on for years to come and serve as an inspiration to subsequent generations of women who want to start their own businesses by putting money into your company, helping other women, giving back to your community, welcoming innovation, and putting an emphasis on sustainability.

CONCLUSION

Become a Woman Billionaire: A Complete Guide to Women's Financial Freedom is a groundbreaking and empowering book that provides a comprehensive roadmap for women who aspire to become financially independent and achieve great success in their careers and businesses.

The book challenges the traditional gender roles and societal norms that have long held women back from realizing their full potential in the world of finance and business. It provides practical and actionable advice on how women can overcome the various obstacles and barriers they may encounter in their pursuit of financial success, including gender bias, imposter syndrome, and lack of access to capital.

The book also offers valuable insights into the latest trends and innovations in the financial industry, such as cryptocurrency and impact investing.

Furthermore, the book emphasizes the importance of financial education, strategic planning, and taking calculated risks to achieve financial freedom. It provides readers with a step-by-step guide to creating a solid financial plan that aligns with their goals and values, including tips on budgeting, saving, investing, and building multiple streams of income.

Finally, "Become a Woman Billionaire" encourages women to support and empower one another in their pursuit of financial success. It recognizes the importance of mentorship, networking, and collaboration in building a strong and supportive community of women who can uplift and inspire one another to achieve greatness.

Overall, "Become a Woman Billionaire" is a valuable resource for any woman who aspires to break through the glass ceiling and achieve financial freedom. It provides a wealth of knowledge, insights, and practical advice that can help women overcome the various challenges they may face and succeed in their quest for financial independence and success. This book is a must-read for any woman who wants to take charge of her financial future and build a life of abundance, impact, and fulfillment.

www.ingramcontent.com/pod-product-compliance
Lightning Source LLC
Chambersburg PA
CBHW060851220526
45466CB00003B/1325